POETRY BY ANTONIA WANG:

Love Bites: Poetry & Prose (2019)

In the Posh Cocoon: Poetry and Bits of Life (2020)

Hindsight 2020: Brief Reflections of a Long Year (2021)

Retrospectiva 2020: Reflexiones Breves Sobre un Año Largo (2021)

Palette: Love Poems and Painted Words (2022)

Things I Could Have Said in One Line But Didn't: Poems on Love,
Relationships and Existentialism (2023)

Matices: Poemas de Amor y Paisajes del Alma (2023)

love bites

POETRY & PROSE
BY ANTONIA WANG

For Patrick & Mia

Contents

"When your **HEART**

quiets your **MIND,** you make it **HOME."**

Part I: Heart

First Draft

In my haste,

I framed the picture

before I painted it.

My life's first draft,

in need of editing,

was carved in stone.

Rebirth, my only recourse,

a dubious prospect—

facets of me in eight dimensions

assemble a clone…

…after your own heart.

Wistfulness

How do you take your coffee

on a rainy day?

I take mine with nutmeg

and torrents of wistfulness.

I aimed futile grasps

at one who fueled my spark;

but flames burn to awaken,

to leave a mark

and subside.

How do you take your coffee,

eons after love made you high?

Lost in Translation

In the verisimilitude of a sequined sky,

you could not trust my love

for a starry night.

Burning amber passion shunned

dense sentiments,

snubbed by the blood-brain barrier.

The best of us was lost in translation.

When you saw me clearly after the fog,

I was long gone.

Palette

There is color under your facade
of monotone brown.
A celeste sky juggles clouds
above your carmine house.
Your eyes are bottle green,
and your lips, carrot.

Your mind, I cannot see.
Its ocean tone is profound.
I won't delve into its trenches,
for I can easily drown.

Serenade

A double rainbow on ashy skies

watched wild horses dash

to the hillside where I met my love.

He woke me up with serenade

at midnight—

with music, his guitar,

and a silver longing that spoke:

I have waited so long to sing you a song

time could not dissolve.

Alchemy

I give you poetic license

to alter the pulsing starlight of my heart.

Craft with infusible steel

an inflorescence.

Transform with the alchemy of your presence

gold gossamers into sage.

Forge in the crucible of your light

an incandescence.

Luna

You know me as the umbral star.
I'm the moody maiden
who only shows at night,
the obscure lover with a hidden side.

I sway oceans with my shapely hips.
I'm a muse to poets, and they amuse me.
My reputation precedes the light.
I'm your companion on lonesome nights.

Lazarus

It has been a while

since I sanded my fingers with your stubble,

since your tormented eyes

made my mouth pout,

and turned gut butterflies into marionettes.

Hush now.

The bolt is jammed,

and the torpid hummingbird in my chest

has died a thousand lives aborning,

calling Lazarus.

Untold

Sit with me.

Some stories are best untold.

You may never know

the paths I walked,

which illusions derailed my soul,

whose sillage lingers on my neck.

It doesn't matter now.

Only we remain,

in the reticence of a starry night.

The Creation of Adam

Let me call you love.

Reality is a blunt reminder of ineffable loss,
of puerile illusions that could not build a home
in dour scars.

The wings meant to help us fly
were consumed at a sports bar,
where our team lost.

We are the near-touching hands
that never entwined.

Apothic

I swam the depths of your turbid waters,
lured by your siren song.

Bioluminous lanterns lit the way.
A trap revealed deceiving prongs.

Intriguing lives lead the bottom feeders,
who serve their banquets in bed.

I choose the ground, where drunkards teeter
on bottles of Apothic red.

The Secret

When water buffalos stampede

to an inch short of your heart,

let them in.

Feelings boomerang

when you throw them out

in a mythos of control.

There is a trick to moving on:

be the fool, widen the door.

And if love spurns you, let it go.

An open heart has no regrets,

and with that knowledge, you forget.

Thrills

Adventures well by the waterfalls,

where delight cascades

from untapped mines of ruby and gold.

Our path unfurls, in thrills we gorge.

Deferred fulfillment falls

to the deep canyons

from which dreams uncurl.

Tricks

In a trick of the light,

I saw blue finches molt on your open eyes.

I watched the sullen moon

weep her sorrows at midnight.

I saw your hands steady my shaky heart,

and the implacable sun making you art.

In a trick of the mind,

I thought you cared.

Cobwebs

I can see you hiding

behind the gossamer veil

of one more delusion,

claiming to soar when you are treading water,

playing peek-a-boo with the inevitable.

I see you consumed by inner fire,

standing next to a river.

I see you through the impotence

of cobwebbed simplicities.

Levity

Take me to a place that's new,

to a meadow where frisson

moves to a slow song

and my lips are fruit.

There is a place

where realized dreams haven't morphed

into loads of burdens.

A place where I'm a stranger,

and you're awash with eyes of wonder.

Cosmic Dance

A hunter looms in the night sky,

harking back to the day we said goodbye.

Time elapsed for two blithe souls,

sullenly shepherded to diverging worlds.

The cosmic dancer stretches his calves,

and breeds felicity in muted laughs.

I taste your joy in a kiss heartfelt,

and tie unknowns with Orion's belt.

Fruitless Pursuits

I have grown espalier to your love,

a vexatious burden of heart,

heightened by being apart.

I overspread in my reach for you—

fruitlessly.

Yet, we're conjoined by the same sun,

nurtured by one moon,

waning regret, waxing hope.

We exist on the same plane,

and for now, that is enough.

Tacit Contract

Break the waves and throw me under.

You already know I'm yours,

as is every shade of green, every hint of blue

emanating from your shores.

This tacit contract won't dissolve

in sporadic encounters.

With you I leave my all,

and return to claim it after hours…

when silence falls.

The Spell

You can peek at the secrets

hidden under my shell,

if you free me from the spell

of this ancient weakness.

It is true I turned away,

but I can no longer see your shadow

under the ghostlight of an old embrace,

and my tears lack eloquence.

There is not much more to say.

Love Bites

Hope

The Japanese maples made it through November,

stunning in fiery red.

Yet our pliant love could not take the fall,

and is hanging by a thread

next to a darkened lake of secrets

concealed by the moon.

A twig of hope lays on the ground,

and a rooting willow looms.

Dream Journal

A deep breath, and I am alone,

far from anything of meaning

but carrying it all inside—

every moment, every ride.

A faint breeze cools me in a Spanish patio,

and a phantasm haunts me.

You watch me across the way,

behind blue curtains red with blood.

I close the shutters, and hear a thud.

Another dream set to replay.

Literal

I ought to learn when "yes" means no,

and "I love you," never.

Vague words knit knots in my literal heart.

I won't seek new starts

in your jumbled dwelling.

Though writing rings compelling

on lyrical doors.

Leave your notes on the floor,

but first, check the spelling.

Lifetimes

Countless lifetimes absent your touch…

Is a century a million kisses,

or an eternity of loss?

Why do overlapping memories

dance not in unison?

Who will fulfill me

for one hundred years

empty of your love?

Stomping Ground

With my child on my hip

on Baker Beach

For horizon, a Golden bridge

Our stomping ground went up in smoke,

bustling still through the fog.

A sudden flash in my mind's eye:

the frigid waters to Alcatraz,

cool sand under my toes,

and your guitar playing on the hill top.

"You used to call me baby.

Now you don't call at all."

Adornment

He wears her nicely to evening galas.

Her demure elegance

is ancillary to his accomplishments—

like the cufflinks and bowtie, a silent adornment.

She is but a motif on his tailored suit,

set aside once they are home.

"Only fools would sacrifice control for intimacy."

She wears gardenias on her lush hair

on a fair afternoon,

unaware of the man.

Wasabi Tears

I am shedding wasabi tears,

for verdant dreams that withered

in a blazing sun of fears;

for hope drowned in a passing storm of tears,

for thoughts that perished with their song inside—

for love so right, nullified.

I am rinsing my mouth with ginger,

to dull the taste of you.

Driftwood Duels

Smells of you in fields of lavender—

inhales of yoga and sandalwood.

Driftwood duels quizzed your caliber

on the road to fatherhood.

A little victory is won each day

in grains of sand from a stormy ocean

that you contain.

Smells of earth, where longings die

and ardors rebirth.

Bulletproof

Those layers,

that add complication but not substance,

that weave knots around a vacuum,

are transparent.

I see you,

a teary child whom life has scorned,

a fragile body a suit has turned

bulletproof.

P.S. Your veneer is melting

under the fire of your hell.

Honorable Discharge

"There was no kill count."

She said, contradicting you.

Yet you battled your share of demons

in that desert storm.

"I don't need that. I have you."

You said, refuting me.

Just another way to hush the mind.

She said you died by accident,

denying you an honorable discharge.

In Memoriam M.R.G.

Moon Gate

I'll meet you at the moon gate,

where passion rages fury beneath our clothes,

where my heart sinks and lifts from a tender hug,

where I can touch your face in tentative bliss—

where I can die the joy of a young love's kiss.

Occupied

"Occupied," reads the sign

on the place you left vacant.

Inside, a void…

Bids withdrawn

by one who prayed for rain,

and ran from storms.

Volcanoes that burned bridges

left fertile land on this ravaged island,

and he planted.

Love's True Fragrance

To approach you

is to get skunked by love,

the toxic stench of adrenaline

and cloudy judgment.

"This will never go away,"

you think, scrubbing your heart

with tomato sauce.

But it will.

Love's true fragrance never stuns.

Phoenix

I found a faded sketch of our life together,
drawn long ago,
when I believed in moving mountains,
and hairy frogs.
I held it to the sun and it combusted.

A baby phoenix emerged from the ashes
and settled on my hand.
"Would you fly with me?"
Alas, I don't know how to fly.
It spit fire and the flames consumed me.
From the ashes I rose, transformed.
"Fly with me," and we soared.

Pending Subjects

Predawn soundscape:

crickets, frogs, birds

and the gnawing susurrus of your voice

bouncing between my ears.

I awaken to muffled echoes,

a mild tug on a heartstring,

a faint nip in my chest

and sticky thoughts that mellowed

in the mortar of time.

Pending subjects linger

like a nursery rhyme.

The Fort

Your heart is a fortress

claimed by many, conquered by none.

Your guards are up

performing rituals,

shooting cannons from miles away,

lest anyone comes close.

Your heart is a fortress

guarding treasures vanished long ago.

Under the Radar

What good is it

to delete what is left of you,

and be put on the radar

of unreasonable attachments

resurfacing under the pretense

of a passing thought?

No. I shall hold dearly to all that remains

of this untold tale.

For everything that reminds me of you

keeps me away from you—

unscathed.

The Red Thread

If memories of you played in my head,

if I remembered your hands caressing my face;

if only I could hear your voice

when I close my eyes.

But all I have is a fragile red thread

that leads to you,

asking me to trust

that a love unseen, unfelt, unproven

will make me whole.

Tokens

These little tokens of you I keep:
a bicycle helmet, a winter hat,
the song you wrote for me,
and your old yoga mat.

Should I ever look back
at a Sierra lush with trees
and see the moving picture
of you smirking on one knee

with a luring invitation:
Wanna play house with me?
I shall hold the fleeting image,
I shall lasso your vestige—

the one that disappears
before I can say: Yes please!

Unstable Orbit

He'd do it.

One last effort to extend his love

A flash of vulnerability to reel her in

A vehement gesture to appease his heart

A final stunt to show she meant everything

And if she didn't acquiesce?

If it wasn't well received,

this would be it. This would be *it!*

Until the next time…

Volcanic Winter

You can smell the sulfur of this volcanic winter.

Words flash-froze in the erupting silence.

Divergence is the only constant

in this simmering rift of wills.

I am here, sweeping the ashes,

wearing a mask.

While you, unfazed by the carnage

of your creative destruction,

reload…

In a Nutshell

Our story hinged

not on the vehemence of my words

but on the weight of yours.

It was you who did not love me first,

or always, or more.

You who should have kept us together

because you couldn't conceive otherwise.

In the end,

it was your ego against mine,

and love flickered.

Justice

Calibrated weights on a scale

delivered the verdict:

unrequited love.

Sentenced to heartbreak,

cease all contact.

Leave all wounds to Dr. Time.

Love serves its time doing push-ups,

and comes out a hunk.

Fools put their trust on a blind lady,

only to wonder what went wrong.

Happiness

Happiness knocked,

dressed in overalls and fancy heels.

Her warmth, foreign,

bred incertitude.

So he chose Loneliness,

a fair maiden.

He was master of his destiny,

and victim of time;

for time stood still in his heart's clock

awaiting Happiness

to spring back to life.

Bonsai

Still-love,

wired into a bonsai…

Under the pebbles,

roots starved of nourishment multiply.

Underground networks

ravel your life once prim,

taking over.

Master gardener, where to trim?

The Portal

The sun burst through the rose window,

revealing bodies of light

speaking songs in ethereal lingo.

Their presence was towering, and lithe.

He stared, hesitant. What is this other side?

Then he saw her tied, and cried.

His promises of "forever"

were naive and blithe.

He stood at a portal of split dimensions,

and all he could do was hide.

Shadow

Your shadow lit me up like a dry forest.

If I shut my eyes, all senses are alive,

and a timid hand massages my scalp.

Your shadow rides country hills,

chasing chimeras on a bike,

wearing a cowboy hat.

I was playing with my hair,

picturing your shadow,

when I saw you in the light.

The Cottage

Cool mornings remind me of

cuddles under a blanket of lust,

late Sunday breakfast,

and a charmed trail of talks.

This vice of mine

of filling the blanks of what could have been;

of storing wishes in the oversoul,

where the two of us dwell

in the cottage of a passing thought—

so in love…

Green Thumb

Everything thrives that you neglect.

The house lily has bore new leaves.

The rose garden is in full bloom,

and this body, waif to your pride

has been recalled from its deathbed

by a tender touch,

lulled by a soft voice that speaks in my ear

when my eyes close.

A Fool's Quest

You left home to find fulfillment,

to quest for one who could

awaken you, revive you, tame you.

Bruised and burned, you return empty handed.

What did the fairy godmother say?

"Love is the trickle that overfills a glass in your

 kitchen sink while you are out chasing rain."

Pineapple Peeling

Pluck my chunks apart.

There is no need to core and slice.

The pattern must not be broken.

There is more than one way

to expose a heart.

Veronica's First Love

Veronica's first love rests in a clay pot

in fluorescent pink,

guarded by azure butterflies.

A handkerchief holds his sweat, and her tears.

Love heads to Calvary

with no messiah to quell its fears.

Ardent nights parted with Eros.

Wash your hands, summon Anteros

to avenge this broken heart.

Ships Passing

He wrote her love letters under The Sun.

His voice,

a ballad of perplexity and sadness,

moved the earth.

A disguise for his face,

a pseudonym for his love…

She couldn't see the rays that warmed her

when he approached her in the night sky.

Foggy Memories

Due North on 101,

I drive through the Headlands' fog

reliving hazy nights at The Fillmore

in a cloud of smoke—

our bobbing to Michael Franti

and his eternal funk.

I descend these hills wrapped in faith.

It is two am. I gaze back at the Golden Gate.

Only a red frame looms

from a lone embrace.

Of Precious Things

"Only the knife knows the pumpkin's heart,"

and you must have seen a pearl

when you carved inside.

Feeling unworthy of such a prize,

you served me on your palm to bystanders

amused by your deed.

You renounced your treasure,

but all *they* saw was a pumpkin seed.

Hound

I chased your scent to Sydney by the Opera House,

ferried from Quay to Manly, swam by a lighthouse.

I smelled you in Madison County

under a covered bridge,

and once again in Willis Tower,

where you were plotting mischief.

I finally got you in Georgia,

sketching the Blue Ridge Mountains.

You smiled and said "Hi love!"

We kissed by the water fountain.

I confronted you, anguished:

"I saw the world for your sake."

You winked before you vanished,

hints of sulfur at your wake.

Little Bribes

Stay,

I'll make home-cooked meals

and save you a spot in bed.

I'll groom you like a monkey,

and rub your pains away.

Stay,

This idyllic vacation is home.

This land, yours,

from the beach to the waterfalls.

Return to the mountains…

Stay,

I'll make you stew and cinnamon rolls.

Part II: Mind

Rose

The fairest rose,

the longest stem

held tightly by the thorns.

Eyes closed,

inhaled its essence…

bouquets of honey and rusty metal.

Rays above me baptized my skin.

Birds below me sampled my blood.

There are creatures that feed on pain.

Nothing is wasted under The Sun.

Metaphors

What if metaphors were true,

and you could summon mountains

with enough certitude,

conjure love out of wishes,

and contact spirits in the rain?

What if life unfolded with your consent,

and years were curves

around the sun's endless bends?

The Now

In the proscenium arch of the day,

time elapses between holidays;

emerging from mental holes,

beribboned in titles and gold.

A child greets the world

immersed in the playground,

while phantom bodies serpentine

foggy paths of doubt.

Hold my water,

while I embrace the now.

Cosmic Prison

I sit,

wet hair dripping,

my back to pine needles

that restrain the undesirable

oblivious to peace lilies that purify the air,

to the vessel of carbon and water

carrying my breath.

I sit

chin up to the cosmic prison

that contains me

in a blanket of freedom.

Sweet Realities

I gift you a box of memories,

amalgam of lives,

souvenirs picked by owls—

who aren't here.

Fresh realities ring surreal

on my right ear.

My heart lags behind a brain

primed for change,

seeking solace every minute.

Grasping is inane.

Monkey Mind

A flame flickers under Buddha's chin.

Piloerection on supple skin,

as you trace your index finger

through the crease of my elbow.

Rainbow pyramids fight a pendulum,

and a citrine cluster over space.

When you blow air on my face,

sweet frisson on veiled eyes.

A wooden coffin burns red roses in a stick.

A monkey mind is in the thick

of Dhyana.

Feelings

Truth hangs in the air,

waiting to be picked

from your choice of cherries,

but the moon is riper.

We orbit the day,

frantic in a dizzying axis.

Myriad reactions prove we are sentient.

Yet, the screens that rule our lives

ran diagnostics.

The algorithm feels we are dead inside.

Calling Card

A key for a door unseen

A gap between

what is known and perceived

 A black hole for illusions

The Architect's calling card

The bird song that sings in your heart

will not be silenced—

or drowned.

The umbilical cord

drawing you back to source

has branded you.

The existential void

Ruminating

Ponder life, the longevity of a vixen

when golden eagles soar.

Being born trimmed your chances.

In beauty there is gore.

The world was yours,

your hastily-devoured oyster plate:

raw, acid, pungent, sweet.

Gone with a blink…

eternal.

Ruminating to understand—

forgot to live.

The Vortex

Dancing to waves,

ripples in time

moving to beats of thought.

Ballerinas draw from the vortex

a simple wish, a fervent dream,

an object feared, neglected joy,

unexpected gifts.

We are walking magnets to a tribe—

all for you, by you.

Twirl to the melody of your song

and pull me in.

ANTONIA WANG

Loss

Release me, sadness, into Morpheus arms!

For I can't mourn, and I won't cry

these little deaths that sting inside:

disappointments, love that starves,

friendships wilting, false starts.

So much loss, so little time,

to deadhead the withered

in a lush summer yard.

Zen

Take one green bean;

eat it slowly.

Lean your head back on the chair.

Trees moon-dance to reggae, mellow.

Sip your Zinfandel, *cielo*[1].

Watch the clouds melt in the night.

Stars are shy, but Sirius.

Breath in deeply, firewood.

A soft spring breeze cools the South.

Crickets to the sky shout.

This is Zen: now.

---

[1] cielo: Spanish for "sky", term of endearment (honey)

ANTONIA WANG

Outwitted

Justice will be served.

Don't taste it.

It's the devil you know vs. Mr. Waste it.

Pick your poison, one is sweeter.

She sits there with a vicious smile

because she fooled you.

The prize she bears is already here.

She called your bluff because she knows

you're too scared to live.

Faith

Falling through the crevasse,

I sense the fungal smell

of things that thrive in the dark.

There are ancient runes carved

with the chisel of a thinking mind.

An untainted lotus in pink

illuminates deep down.

Its leaves are lacquered in faith,

and ribbons of gratitude swathe its crown.

The Word

To magnify reality is to transcend it.

God created poetry out of dark matter.

For that which can't be overcome

must be transmuted into art.

Poetry is the pixie dust of life.

Words are cheap. Words are invaluable.

Reasons

I write, not because the pen is my friend,

and words flow to my brain

in rhythmic patterns of wonder and grace.

I write, not because I'm skilled,

my veil translucent, nor do I have musings.

What I have is a screaming urge that nags me

to birth a child out of reverie:

eloquent diction, channelled love

or clumsy clumps of awkward thought.

I write simply, because I must.

ANTONIA WANG

Poet

Strip layers of meaning

to discover the rhyme.

Galloping the folds of time,

a poet is dreaming.

Her pouch hides obscure pearls

from a rushing river:

of her heart, a sliver;

of her mind, curls;

for her pleasure, words—

her muse delivers.

Empathy

If you can feel the joy of a morning glory,

and the grief of a mourning dove;

if you shed the tears of a weeping willow,

and hurt with the bloody moon;

if you run from a tiger lily,

and sit on a cloud of bats—

you have the empathy of a poet,

and the agility of an acrobat.

Nursing Dreams

Torrential downpours are seen through the frame

of floor to ceiling windows.

A vacant play set conjures children.

Dreams are conceived in the maelstrom

of an urban womb lain dormant.

Yearning saplings whistle in a nursery,

roots to soil, leaves perked up,

expecting your touch.

Dark Angel

Who will cry for the jilted prince,

who loved at his own peril after losing the girl,

who dealt with evil in self-sacrifice,

was snaped[2] as a villain,

and paid the ultimate price?

Who had his wings severed,

his life painted black

and his slithering tears

collected in a flask?

---

[2] (hint: Severus Snape)

ANTONIA WANG

Red Rooster

I lie left on the bed, as if to crush the heart.

My muse is a mule who balks at love,

but is moved by a spider plant.

A red rooster sits on my roof eating fried okra.

Resplendent feathers are part of his ruse

to steal a sip of vodka—

standing upright, as if to lift the heart.

Choose Joy

The sun hides when the moon shines

and you wear your badge of pain.

It is your name tag and your shield.

What evil haunts us today?

There is no relief for shared troubles.

Hurt is ubiquitous on this plane.

There is jubilation in non-attachment—

suffering's troubling bane.

The Sun

The Sun can't hide, stop shining,

or be eclipsed with a finger.

It can't be wished away,

or replaced with an impostor.

The Sun can't help

but don its rays upon the earth,

making things grow

and eventually decay.

Reflection

Beneath this roof,

memories compete for space on wall shelves:

photos, figurines, seashells.

The sun bursts through a concave mirror,

showing me pictures of what life could be.

A nude woman reflects across the way.

With her eyes closed, she looks within,

smiling widely back at me.

Part III: Home

Rubio

There are paw prints on my yoga mat,

and claw-sized holes from my stretchy cat.

He bites my ankles in downward dog,

and kneads my back during painful frog.

I love this curious creature

who wreaks havoc under my nose.

He lacks the loyalty of a terrier,

and the empathy of a rose.

Mother

Kids floss under a raining hose.

How high can water go?

The sponge is wet.

Throw it up.

Curvy hips have reached their zenith.

Fanny packs are jammed with Kleenex.

So much beauty clad in black

under a hot sun.

Child

I can stunt the dragons

that stymie your growth.

I can pull you from the rabble

and dissect your thoughts.

I can stake palisades around you

with the fury of a thousand hulks;

but I cannot protect you

from the temerity of your own heart.

Be resilient, be wise.

Morning Cadence

Birds murmur on a rooftop

about protein shakes for breakfast.

Lips peck, and a yellow bus

salutes the morning cadence.

One more ride around the sun—

no happy endings, just quirky songs.

One, two, three, four…

A cat stares out the window.

A frog's dilemma:

to jump or not to jump

Mundanity

Sweet nuts to roast sanity,

a cat who plays guitar.

Salty caramels scream mundanity,

bits of lipstick raise the bar.

Yard frogs of various species

sing happy songs—

of carefully washed butter knives.

An iron upright contains the spills,

and the vapid thrills

of domestic life.

The Vase

We gather shells from every beach

and bring them home.

Our anthology of mementos

was cured with sea foam…

waves of existence washed by the tide,

oceans of life in a vase.

Water is our point of reference.

Its coolness, inviting. Its depth, safe.

Like crabs, fleeing crumbling holes

to be in their element,

we ghost the night.

Crimson Queen

Four Japanese maples

are ritually planted in every place.

This solemn baptism is a wish,

not a promise to stay.

Two cardinals perch and glide,

striking tango

between growing roots

and fate manifest.

A house to the east, home to the west.

Are we the maples, or birds seeking rest?

The Grotto

The mother from the grotto hugs me gently,

while kids ring around the rosie near.

"You will go far from here."

In vague recollection, I see one tear,

crystal clear, wet her porcelain cheek.

"This town is too small, your hopes too big.

Fly child. Leave me here. I will find you in your dreams."

I returned to the grotto twenty years later.

"I'm back mother. The town has grown."

She flashes me a faint smile,

as though I should have known…

"No dear, you have."

Porcelain Doll

She twirls in a gingham dress.

"Momma won't let me dance in the rain

or swim in the river, ride a bike, or curl my hair.

Dating is a dare."

Raised in a bubble, above the muck

a porcelain doll braves a loathsome world;

but she could only see lilies, she could only smell love.

Now she rides nude in quiet roar.

Her unruly mane sways to a cadenced wind,

and her carmine lips part in a wide grin.

The Other Side of Love

The faces of innocence:

a rare tribe who only knew decency—

their clear gaze, that honest smile

a riddle to those

on the other side of love.

Gentle now,

for they don't know your growing pains.

Bask in their light, pet their tenderness.

Touch them gingerly

with two fingers.

Dad

Tedious days on the hamster wheel

exercise futility.

The truth du jour is pinned by the door,

while twin bulbs choke at the neck

of a winged hourglass.

Fine sand slips through my fingers;

but your ephemeral smile was captured

by a heart raised with kindness,

bolstered by love unending.

Fragrant

In fragrant death of rosemary and lavender,

your smile lives on my shelves,

long after the days unfolded

and silence fell.

You reach out when I despair

in the folly of a weakened heart.

You roam the heavens while I'm alive.

Who can belittle me, when you called me a star?

Who can break me after you[3] loved me?

---

[3] In loving memory of Blas Suriel

Love Bites

Amparo

She picked coffee beans on her family farm,

only from the bottom to prevent any harm.

She washed clothes on river rocks with glycerin soap.

She walked many miles to pray to her God.

She sang with the choir when she met my dad.

With aplomb, they built a home that still stands.

Her tender eyes are azure like the clear sky.

Her beatific hands, healing as balm.

I will loan her to you, but only for a day

if you need a mom.

The Bride

Your life is a symbol, your truth, a veil

of renounced passions and forfeited childhoods

relived in a school yard.

A bride in white,

down on your knees at the crack of dawn,

paying dues to love;

confined to a harem of snakes that strike

while bowing to their King,

in fervor.

Under the Saman

At the town square, sitting under The Saman,

a boy asks if I need my shoes shined.

He readies his dirty rag and polish paste.

I wonder who his parents are,

what troubles he's faced.

Sitting under an old tree

on a Sunday afternoon,

I learned to count my blessings.

ANTONIA WANG

The Sacristan

I sip wine in the sacristy on Saturday mornings,

while watching the door.

I dust endless pews,

sweep and mop the marble floors.

My father tends metal shutters

twelve feet above.

There are always flowers for Mary.

I want to take one home.

I got pennies for my sweat,

and myriad lessons

about the sanctity of work

from a man I adored.

Quisqueya

If I close my eyes I see green mountains,

white sand beaches,

and coconut groves.

My hips swing to bachata

craving blond roast coffee and rum,

sugar cane and *tostones*[4],

cacao beans and mum.

I'm pregnant with nostalgia.

Quisqueya[5] calls me home.

---

4 *Tostones*: fried, green plantains.

5 *Quisqueya*: native Taino name for the island of Hispaniola

Eagle's Bay

Placid bay water lulls you in a sultry embrace.

Sunshine bounces off silver-scaled sardines

nibbling your feet.

Not a soul around you…

Due North—

fields of dwarf palms, and Canelilla shrubs.

Due South—

the vivid horizon imposes,

and Yemoja[6] lures you home.

---

[6] Yemoja is the African goddess of the ocean, referenced in Afro-Caribbean folklore.

Love Bites

Golden History

Caonabo[7], handle your people!

They are exchanging gold for mirrors.

Those are not bracelets but handcuffs.

Columbus is a thief, not a hero.

I am the Spaniards and the French

who ransacked this peaceful island.

I am the immigrants and African slaves

from whose ribs two countries emerged.

I am the Taino, all but extinct who fled

to the Maguana highlands. Europeans

and greedy explorers all panned for their pay day.

My history is an eclectic totem,

and it is written in my DNA.

---

[7] Caonabo was the indigenous Taino chief of the Maguana Chiefdom, one of five on the island of Hispaniola at the time of the Spaniards' arrival in 1492.

About the Author

Antonia Wang is the author of Love Bites, In the Posh Cocoon, Hindsight 2020, *Retrospectiva 2020*, *Matices*, Palette, and Things I Could Have Said in One Line But Didn't. She is an international CASS scholar originally from the Dominican Republic. Her work has been praised for its vibrant imagery and thoughtful exploration of themes such as love, loss, personal transformation and identity. Her distinctive poetic voice appears in several literary journals and anthologies. She writes in English and Spanish.

Antonia draws inspiration from her world travels, Caribbean heritage, and long-standing yoga practice. She lives with her family in the United States.

Website: biteslove.com

Acknowledgments

Special thanks to Princess Yvonne Dumas (@WritingByPrin), for editing this collection with a keen eye for detail.

My deep appreciation to the #vss365 writing prompt organizers on Twitter, to the writing community, and everyone who inspires and supports my poetry online and offline.

All my love and gratitude to my family, for the myriad ways they support my writing journey.

Thank you for reading!

If you enjoyed Love Bites, please take a moment to *review it*. Your feedback is important to me, and it helps other readers find this book.

Made in the USA
Las Vegas, NV
29 January 2024